LIGHTNING BOLT BOOKS™

Meet a Baby Gray Wolf

Tamika M. Murray

Lerner Publications ◆ Minneapolis

For the Gray Wolves

Lerner Publications Company
An imprint of Lerner Publishing Group, Inc.
241 First Avenue North
Minneapolis, MN 55401 USA

For reading levels and more information, look up this title at www.lernerbooks.com.

Main body text set in Billy Infant Regular. Typeface provided by SparkType.

Library of Congress Cataloging-in-Publication Data

Names: Murray, Tamika M., author.
Title: Meet a baby gray wolf / Tamika M. Murray.
Description: Minneapolis : Lerner Publications, [2024] | Series: Lightning bolt books - baby North American animals | Includes bibliographical references and index. | Audience: Ages 6-9 | Audience: Grades 2-3 | Summary: "Learn all about the baby gray wolf! From when they walk to what they eat, readers will catch a fun and engaging glimpse of the early lives of gray wolves"— Provided by publisher.
Identifiers: LCCN 2022035596 (print) | LCCN 2022035597 (ebook) | ISBN 9781728491110 (library binding) | ISBN 9781728498300 (ebook)
Subjects: LCSH: Gray wolf—North America—Juvenile literature.
Classification: LCC QL737.C22 M865 2024 (print) | LCC QL737.C22 (ebook) | DDC 599.773097—dc23/eng/20220726

LC record available at https://lccn.loc.gov/2022035596
LC ebook record available at https://lccn.loc.gov/2022035597

Manufactured in the United States of America
1-53042-51060-9/23/2022

Table of Contents

Life of a Gray Wolf Pup

The den is hidden and quiet. A gray wolf gives birth to a pup. It grew inside her for about two months. A newborn pup weighs about 1 pound (0.5 kg). That is about the same as a box of cereal.

An adult female wolf is a she-wolf. She usually has four to six pups in a litter. She nurses her pups inside the den.

Pups cannot hear or see at birth. Their eyes open after ten to fifteen days.

Pups are still small when they open their eyes.

They begin to crawl then too. But they don't stand or walk until they are fourteen to twenty-four days old.

Living in a Pack

Gray wolf pups live in a pack. Most packs have four to nine wolves. The pack includes the mom and dad wolf. In a pack, only one pair of wolves mates and has pups.

The pups can make sounds such as howls when they are two to three weeks old. Wolves howl to communicate with one another.

A pup howling to other pack members

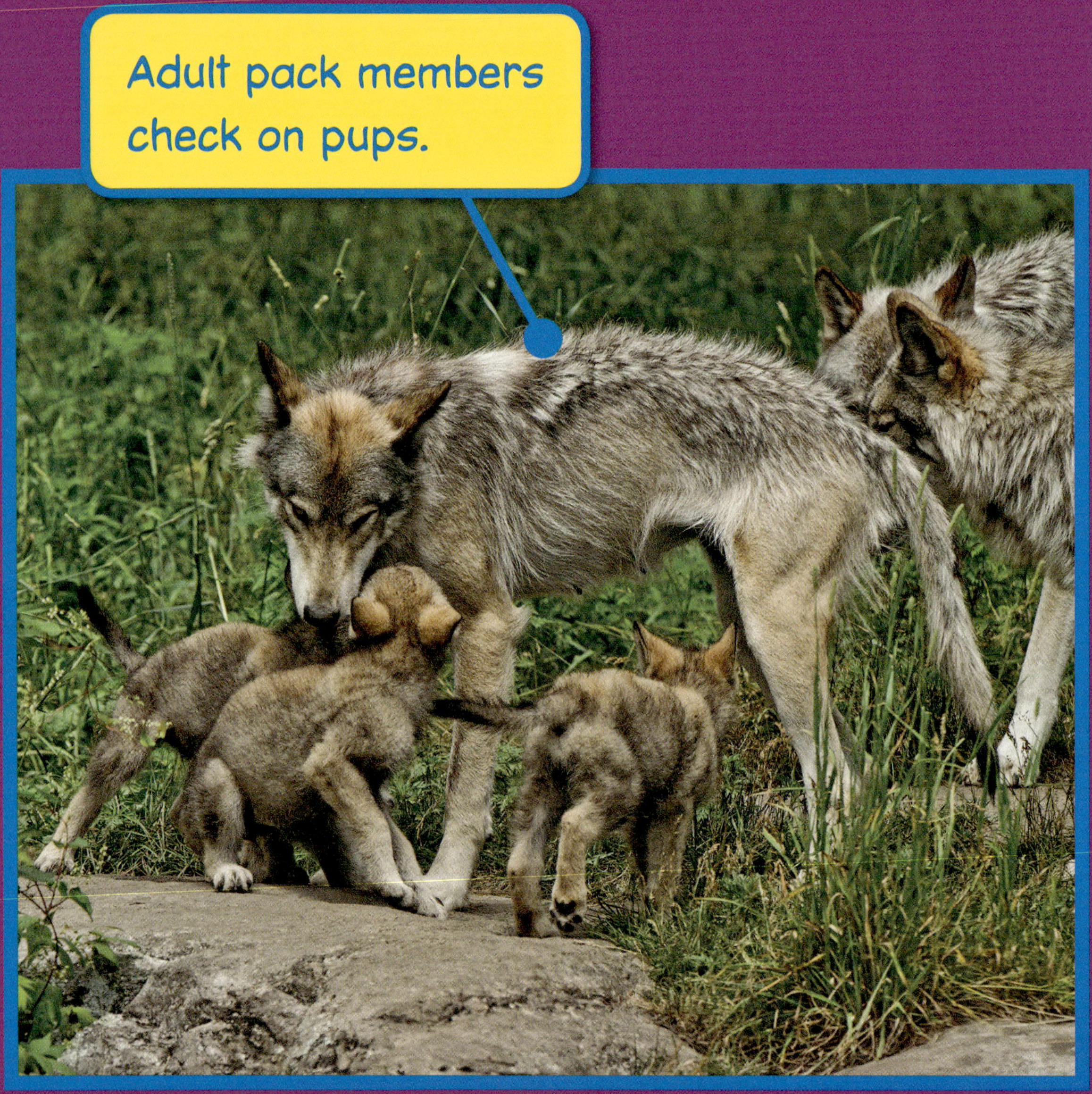

Living in a pack provides safety. The whole pack helps keep the pups safe from predators.

The pack protects adult members too. Coyotes, other wolves, and humans are gray wolves' main predators.

A wolf pack protects adults and pups.

Milk and Meals

Between days twenty-four and seventy-seven, pups begin to leave the den. They play fight and sleep while the adults hunt.

A pup eating

The she-wolf nurses her pup for six to nine weeks. Then the pups are weaned.

Gray wolves are carnivores. They eat meat. Other wolves chew meat for pups when they are first weaned. They start hunting at six or seven months.

Pups grow up fast. They reach almost adult size in about six months. Adult males weigh 70 to 145 pounds (32 to 66 kg). Females weigh 60 to 100 pounds (27 to 45 kg).

Growing Up

A gray wolf decides where to live when it is two to three years old. Some wolves stay in the pack. But others leave to start their own packs.

Gray wolves live about six to eight years in the wild. But some wild wolves can live up to ten or more years! And they can live even longer in captivity.

Gray wolves often live longer in captivity.

After choosing to stay or leave the pack, a gray wolf looks for a mate. A she-wolf can have pups around the age of two years.

A male and a female wolf nuzzling

Gray wolves have pups every spring. Then the pups grow up and start a family of their own.

Gray Wolf Life Cycle

Habitat in Focus

- In North America, gray wolves live in parts of Canada and the US.
- A pack's territory can be 31 to 1,158 square miles (80 to 3,000 sq. km).
- A pack travels to different areas within its territory to hunt.

Fun Facts

- A gray wolf can eat up to 20 pounds (9 kg) of meat during one meal.
- Gray wolves communicate by touching chins and rolling over to show off their stomachs.
- Gray wolves can run up to 36 to 38 miles (58 to 61 km) per hour.
- Gray wolves usually travel at night.
- Gray wolves often stay with the same mate for their adult life.

Glossary

captivity: to be held somewhere without being able to leave

carnivore: an animal that eats meat

den: a place such as a cave or hole where a female gray wolf gives birth and raises the pups for the first three months

litter: a group of pups

mate: one of a pair of animals that are breeding

pack: a group of gray wolves that lives and hunts together

predator: an animal that preys on other animals

wean: when an animal stops drinking its mother's milk

Learn More

Britannica Kids: Wolf
https://kids.britannica.com/kids/article/wolf/353930

Fun Wolf Facts
https://wolf.org/wolf-info/wild-kids/fun-facts/

Herrington, Lisa M. *Gray Wolves*. New York: Children's Press, 2019.

Murray, Julie. *Dens*. Minneapolis: Abdo Kids Junior, 2020.

National Geographic Kids: Gray Wolf
https://kids.nationalgeographic.com/animals/mammals/facts/gray-wolf

Schwartz, Heather E. *Meet a Baby Beaver*. Minneapolis: Lerner Publications, 2024.

Index

Photo Acknowledgments

Image credits: John Pitcher/Getty Images, pp. 4, 19; Sylvain Cordier/Getty Images, p. 5; Alexey Osokin/Getty Images, p. 6; Anita Erdmann/Alamy Stock Photo, pp. 7, 19; Geoffrey Kuchera/Shutterstock, p. 8; twildlife/Getty Images, p. 9; Michael Cummings/Getty Images, p. 10; Robert Pickett/Getty Images, p. 11; Zocha_K/Getty Images, p. 12; blickwinkel/Alamy Stock Photo, p. 13; imageBROKER/Alamy Stock Photo, p. 14; Andy_Astbury/Getty Images, p. 15; USO/Getty Images, p. 16; JJAF/Getty Images, p. 17; Diane Picard/Shutterstock, p. 18; Stan Tekiela/Getty Images, p. 19; Laura Westlund, p. 20.

Cover credit: Lynn_Bystrom/Getty Images.